NATURAL OF THE

Published by Gallery Books
A Division of W H Smith Publishers Inc.
112 Madison Avenue
New York, New York 10016

Produced by
Bison Books Corp.
15 Sherwood Place
Greenwich, CT 06830

ISBN 0-8317-6332-9

Printed in Hong Kong

1 2 3 4 5 6 7 8 9 10

TREASURES WEST

PHOTOGRAPHY	MIREILLE VAUTIER ALINE DE NANXE
TEXT	ROBIN LANGLEY SOMMER
DESIGN	MIKE ROSE

GALLERY BOOKS
An imprint of W.H. Smith Publishers Inc.
112 Madison Avenue
New York, New York 10016
A Bison Book

The photograph on page 115 was provided courtesy of
Canadian Springs Hotel, Banff Springs Hotel; the
photograph on page 110 was provided courtesy of the
Government of British Columbia; the photograph on
pages 118-19 was provided courtesy of Travel Alberta.
The following photographs were supplied by Photo/Graphics
Stock Library, North Vancouver, British Columbia: 123
(Derek and Jane Abson), 121 (John Burridge), 122,
124-25 (Bob Herger), 120, 126 (Gunter Marx) and
117 (Richard Wright).

*3-6 A panoramic view of the Pinnacles in
Badlands National Park, South Dakota.*

INTRODUCTION

Little more than a hundred years ago, the western wilderness of North America was terra incognita to most people. Its natural wonders were known mainly to the widely scattered native Americans of the pueblos, plains and forests. The first intrepid explorers of the Far West returned to civilization with tales that were scarcely credible: of vast monoliths looming abruptly over desolate flatlands; arid deserts dotted with startling and exotic plants and animals; volcanic mountain ranges mantled in rivers of ice; torrential waterways that cut sheer chasms through living stone to unimaginable depths. These tales seemed so fantastic and even contradictory that they were slow to gain credence among residents of the less spectacular and long-settled Eastern Seaboard. But as more and more people found themselves feeling crowded, and succumbed to the lure of new, wider horizons, the treasures of the West became increasingly better known and appreciated.

John Muir, the Scottish-born naturalist whose passionate love of nature was shared by President Theodore Roosevelt, published the wonders of wild Glacier Point, where he and Roosevelt camped together and formed the resolve to preserve the whole Yosemite Valley for posterity. Muir's tireless travels through the West brought public awareness of the wilderness heritage from the Sierra Nevada to the Pacific Northwest. The adventurous Major

John Wesley Powell, who had lost an arm in the Civil War, led a bold expedition down the turbulent Colorado River in 1869. Two of his four boats were lost, but his whole party survived to spread new knowledge of the Southwest, which had been largely a question mark to cartographers until this time. As a result of this and other forays into the unknown, Powell was given the directorship of the newly formed Smithsonian Institution, which has done so much to preserve America's past.

For the most part, however, the wonders west of the Continental Divide were discovered by ordinary people: prospectors, trappers, settlers and mountain men. The Mormon settlers of Utah explored and named the convoluted rainbow-colored canyons and striated domes of rock that now comprise Bryce Canyon and Mount Zion National Parks. Soon after, others whose names are unknown to us were the first white men to see the steaming fountains, springs and terraces of Yellowstone, where Wyoming, Montana and Idaho converge; the Petrified Forest of Arizona; the soaring stone arches of eastern Utah; the ancient cliff dwellings of Colorado's Mesa Verde. Some tried to capture their experiences in letters and journals; others sought to convey it in words that seemed always inadequate. But one did not have to be either literate or articulate to respond to the endless plains and dizzying heights of the immense new land.

In all the varied sights of the Far West, there was only one constant: change. These scenic wonders had been formed by great convulsions of nature— volcanic upheavals from the fiery heart of the earth, vast tectonic movements far below its surface, thunderous glaciers that swept mountains and forests before them. Hand in hand with these dramatic upheavals were the slow, implacable forces of erosion, by wind, water, frost, snow and falling rock. In the Grand Canyon of the Colorado, two billion years of earth's history can be traced from the black rock of the inner gorge—the Vishnu Schist—to the highest rim rocks, where Kaibab Limestone holds fossils of the last trilobites, which lived in a shallow sea. These are the canyon's youngest rocks—280 million years old—deposited as sand by an inflowing sea long before the dinosaurs walked here.

Some 80 million years later, this was a subtropical land—a vast floodplain bordered on the South and West by active volcanoes. Luxuriant tree ferns, ginkgo trees and 40-foot ancestors of today's horsetail fringed great swamps and sluggish waterways that were home to the earliest forerunners of the dinosaurs. Crocodile-like phytosaurs weighing several tons prowled the shallow waters in search of prey, which included, perhaps, the fish-eating metoposaurs, some of the largest amphibians that ever lived. Ranging the land was the rapacious, fast-running carnivore called *Lythrodynastes,* or 'gore lord,' which could travel on all four legs or rear up on two like the later tyrannosaurs. Fossil remains of these and other long-vanished species provide clues to life in the Far West before the Rocky Mountains thrust skyward, the Colorado Plateau was uplifted and the buried floodplain, washed of younger sediments by erosion, was restored to the earth's surface.

Later chapters of this story in stone are written in the walls of Utah's Bryce Canyon and Zion, several hundred miles to the North. As the Colorado Plateau rose, south side first, quiet streams like the Colorado River and its tributaries ran faster, undercutting whole layers of rock to leave a 200-mile series of south-facing cliffs—the Grand Staircase—that represents another 15 million years of geological history. Each row of cliffs, named for the distinctive color of rock that it displays, exposes a different time period, from the Chocolate Cliffs just north of the Grand Canyon to the Pink Cliffs of Bryce's iron-rich rock. The relentless forces of erosion are still at work today, from the rapidly eroding clay Badlands of South Dakota to the harder formations of the Grand Canyon, whose rate of erosion is less than an inch every hundred years.

Long after the land itself took shape, man appeared in the West. Asiatic hunters crossed the Bering Strait when it was a land bridge and fanned out across the North American continent. The western peoples evolved distinctive ways of life, ranging from that of the fishermen along the Northwest Coast to the pueblo villagers, farmers and nomads of the Southwest. Between them were the California-Intermountain tribes, occupying the dry plateaus and deserts between the Sierra Nevada and the Rockies. All have left their imprint on the land in the form of place names, petroglyphs, cave paintings, artifacts, terraced pueblos and fossil remains that help archaeologists tie together the past and present of America's native peoples.

But the Far West is much more than a living textbook for scientists. Most of those who seek out its sweeping vistas and secluded oases are looking for the spiritual and emotional renewal that comes from re-establishing one's ties with nature—ties that have been sundered by the frenetic pace of contemporary society. Time stands still for a fisherman in a shady trout pool, or a determined hiker scaling one more ridge to see what new beauty it conceals. For these and millions like them, many natural treasures of the West have been preserved by conservationists, lawmakers and citizens of vision. They remain much as they were when western artist George Catlin recorded his impressions on a spring day in 1832, 'in all the wild and freshness of their nature's beauty!' These realms of peaceful grandeur help to restore our awareness of the unity and continuity of all life, and awaken us to the communal task of preserving the earth that is our home.

ROBIN LANGLEY SOMMER

CANYONS AND MESAS

The canyons and mesas of the West, especially the Grand Canyon of the Colorado, are among the natural wonders of the world. Even the most remote and inaccessible of them have been brought within reach of hikers, riders and campers who want to explore and test themselves against these challenging environments. Others are content to view them from various points along the rim. From either vantage point, one's efforts will be rewarded by such vistas as few other regions of the world can offer.

The multicolored and fantastically shaped formations of Utah's Bryce Canyon, some 60 million years old, overlie much older rocks which have become visible in nearby Zion Canyon, where majestic, delicately tinted sandstone cliffs rise more than 3000 feet toward the blue arc of the sky. Much of the rock here is porous, and multiple waterfalls spring to life after a rain. Bryce, by contrast, is almost totally arid: the Paiute Indian name for it could be translated as 'red rocks standing like men in a bowl-shaped canyon.' A seed-gathering people, the Paiutes found little food here, but they encamped for the summer on the Paunsaugunt Plateau above the canyon, where they collected the pinon nuts that were a staple of their diet.

The fairytale landscape of Bryce Canyon was once the floor of an inland sea. Then massive pressure from within the earth thrust up a huge mesa along deep faults. Rain, wind and frost gradually wore away the edges of this tabletop formation into the strange spires, pinnacles, bridges and standing stones that exist today. The canyon is named for its first white settler, a Mormon immigrant from Scotland named Ebenezer Bryce, who described it more prosaically than his Indian predecessors: he called it 'a hell of a place to lose a cow.'

Uplift and erosion were also the principal architects of the Grand Canyon, which began as a plain through which a quiet river cut a shallow bed. As subterranean forces lifted the plain,in a cataclysmic upheaval that sundered the entire Southwest, the river flowed faster and cut deeper. Over the centuries it dug a chasm some 200 miles long, averaging nine miles wide and over a mile deep. The great depth of this canyon affects temperature and precipitation to such a degree that the life forms occurring down its walls at various points represent the entire range of the North American continent. Near the level of the river are desert plants and animals typical of Mexico's Sonora, including rattlesnakes, lizards and yucca. Higher up, as the climate cools, are life forms typical of the northern United States. Higher still, on both North and South Rims, are the Douglas fir, aspen and blue grouse common to Canadian forests, while North Rim elevations above 9000 feet are as cold as Hudson's Bay.

Capitol Reef, in southcentral Utah, is another monument to the forces of nature. Here the earth thrust up a great ridge of sandstone, whose brightly colored layers have been eroded by wind and water into tortuous canyons, natural bridges and cisterns, and giant domes. Mormon settlers once raised crops and herded cattle here along the Fremont River, and many beautiful fruit trees remain to flower with the wild sego lilies in late spring.

15 The eerily beautiful formations of Bryce Canyon resemble a moonscape except for their vivid coloring.

16-17 Canyon de Chelly National Monument, Arizona, preserves the ruins of prehistoric Indian villages in caves below its sheer red cliffs.

18-19 A sudden storm gathers over Bryce Canyon.

20 Pink pinnacles of fantastically eroded limestone guard the mazelike ravines of Bryce Canyon.

21 top The Navajo called the ramparts of multicolored rock at Capitol Reef, Utah, 'Land of the Sleeping Rainbow.'

21 bottom An astonished surveyor described the canyon in 1876 as 'The wildest and most wonderful scene that the eye of man ever beheld.'

22-23 A table-like mesa towers over Arizona's incredible Grand Canyon of the Colorado.

24 Campers are attracted to the rugged landscape of Red Rock Canyon State Park in California.

25 Hikers get a closer look at Bryce Canyon's strange formations than those who view them from the rim.

26-27 Two billion years of earth's history are written in the rocks of the Grand Canyon.

28 The Grand Canyon takes on a luminous quality
under a darkening sky.

29 The landscape of Bryce Canyon is
everchanging with the varying light of day.

DUNES AND DESERTS

Man has always had a fascination for the stark simplicity of the desert, where survival is the only imperative. The desert's harsh, unvarying landscape, its pitiless heat and frigid nights, can be implacable foes or allies, depending upon what one seeks there.

Historically, men have gone into the desert to find freedom—in a nomadic existence that flows with the shifting winds and sands, or in a solitary quest for one's own identity, far from the attachments and demands of society. Others have seen the desert only as a vast and forbidding obstacle in their paths, and many have perished in the attempt to conquer it. California's Death Valley was named by the pioneers who survived the crossing of it in 1849, and other place names there testify to the desolation they experienced—Bad Water, Funeral Mountain, Black Mountain.

But for those who are attuned to its unique beauties, and compliant to its demands, the desert is an enthralling place. Its apparent sterility is only a veil drawn over the abundant life that it generates and sustains. Patience alone can surprise many of the desert's creatures, whose life goes on beneath the ever-changing, rippled dunes or under cover of darkness. There plants and animals conspire together for survival. The bristling cholla provides a congenial hiding place for nesting cactus wrens, although most animals shun its painful barbed spines. Kangaroo rats emerge from their burrows at dusk to forage seeds from the bell-flowered yucca; these and other seeds contain the only water they will ever drink. Pocket mice, hares and rabbits, spadefoot toads and sidewinders all leave their ephemeral traces in the sand. The howl of a hunting coyote is one of the few sounds to break the silence of the desert night.

The American Southwest has thousands of square miles of desert, including White Sands National Monument in southern New Mexico, whose blown gypsum sand can resemble a vast snowfield. Arizona boasts the brilliantly colored Painted Desert, along the Little Colorado River, and California has the Mojave Desert, north of Baja, which once lay beneath the Pacific Ocean. In Monument Valley, the Navajo Indians hold to their traditional way of life, raising sheep for food and wool for use in weaving. Their handicrafts and works of art, including beautiful sand paintings of ritual significance, evolve from the arid land they live in. Unlike the white settlers, who saw the desert as an enemy, its native people revere it and accommodate themselves to its demands.

Early peoples of the Southwest included the Anasazi, or Ancient Ones, who built cliff dwellings in what is now northern Arizona, New Mexico, Utah and Colorado; the Hohokam, who dug extensive irrigation canals to farm Arizona's scantily watered land; and the Mogollon, who were hunters and farmers in this region. Desert soils are usually very fertile, and where irrigation from a river or by means of wells is possible, the ground becomes very productive, as in California's Imperial Valley. Thus much Southwestern desert land has been made arable. But vast tracts will remain in their natural state through the National Park System and other conservation-minded organizations which realize their importance as part of the wilderness heritage. For those who know how to appreciate it, the desert is anything but lifeless.

31 The infrequent rains of California's Death Valley dry rapidly into depressions that resemble fossil footprints.

32 Cholla cacti bristle in the Colorado Desert.

33 The tenacious Joshua Tree is a member of the
yucca family.

34-35 *Death Valley's shifting, sand-sculpted dunes are preserved as a National Monument.*

36-37 *Desert winds form patterns reminiscent of a Japanese gardener's carefully raked sand paths.*

38-39 A solitary soaptree yucca dominates this vista in White Sands National Park, New Mexico.

40 Claret cup cacti flourish in Arizona's arid Monument Valley, ancestral home of the Navajo Indians.

41 Flowering yucca and the delicate desert mallow in bloom.

42-43 Southeastern California's great Mojave Desert lies between the Sierra Nevada (snow-covered mountain range) and the Colorado River.

44 Erosion carves the soft sandstone of the Mojave into weird formations.

45 A few hardy desert plants cling to the memory
of rainfall in Death Valley.

46-47 The desert horizon at Death Valley seems
to recede into infinity.

48 The solitude of the desert exerts its primal
attraction on those in search of respite from the
complexities of urban life.

49 Riding trails lead the adventurous into the heat-shimmering heart of Bryce Canyon.

50-51 Moonlike Death Valley was a large lake in glacial times.

MAN AND NATURE

Man has left his imprint on the West since prehistoric times, when the first nomadic hunters took shelter in caves and drew human and animal figures on the rocky walls. The Anasazi built rudimentary cliff dwellings in what is now southeastern Utah, marking a turn away from the nomadic life toward a more settled abode. The first constructions were little more than rude huts that covered storage pits, with mud used as mortar. Later, at Mesa Verde, Colorado, these squat, semicircular structures were replaced with increasingly elaborate apartments built with stone masonry techniques in the shelter of overhanging cliffs. An advanced culture of the early pueblo (village) type flourished at Mesa Verde between AD 750 and 1300.

The Mesa Verdes—often called the Basket Makers—were skillful weavers and farmers. In time they became adept at making pottery, and grew corn, beans and squash in fields below the cliff houses. Water was brought into the fields from nearby springs. They developed an extensive trade network that included tribes as far away as the coast of California, from whom they obtained shells. Other pueblo tribes farther south provided them with turquoise and with cotton for textile weaving. The produce they grew with such effort in their dry environment was supplemented by hunting.

Ground corn was the Mesa Verdes' staple food, and a prolonged drought may have been one of the factors that led them to abandon the community here around AD 1300. Other possible causes may have been exhaustion of the soil and depletion of game animals and firewood, never plentiful in the Southwest. Whatever the reasons, the people left their great stone houses and the mysterious Sun Temple that crowns the mesa: they have been untenanted for 700 years. The longevity of the ruins here is a testimony to the skill of their builders.

Early white settlers, in turn, left their mark on the land, for good and ill. The Spaniards introduced the horse into the New World, and hunters of the plains and desert swiftly incorporated this new beast of burden into their way of life. The horse was one of very few benefits conferred by the white man, whose incursions would eventually crowd the native peoples into desolate reservations, or decimate their ranks through warfare and diseases to which they had no immunity.

Land and gold fever, furs and forests, brought ever-greater numbers of settlers into the Far West throughout the nineteenth century. Abandoned ghost towns still stand near the site of empty mines, or on land that proved too harsh and difficult for farming and herding. Many frontier towns that sprang up in response to the impetus of westward migration fell into rubble once their purpose was accomplished—a railroad completed, a mine played out. Crude frame dwellings tenanted only by tumbleweed, deserted mineshafts and rusted rail lines mark these sites.

Other frontier settlements grew into prosperous communities that are major cities today—Denver, San Francisco, Salt Lake City. They provide the best of both worlds: a stimulating urban environment with ready access to a more leisurely way of life in a beautiful natural setting. Much depended— and still depends—on the quality of the relationship between man and nature, whether hostile and exploitative on man's part, or appreciative, caring and conserving.

53 A weathered remnant of boom times in Bowie, California, now a ghost town.

54-55 One of the famous 20-mule-team wagons once used in mining borax in Death Valley.

56 top Wolfe Ranch in Arches National Park, settled by hard-working Mormon pioneers.

56 bottom Iron-wheeled wagons jolted early settlers through the town of Bodie.

57 A Navajo dwelling in the tribal park at Monument Valley, Arizona, part of the 96,000-acre Navajo reservation.

58-59 A graceful serpentine boardwalk is a harmonious element in its natural setting at Yellowstone.

60-61 Mount Rushmore National Monument, in South Dakota's Black Hills, is a massive memorial to Presidents Washington, Jefferson, Lincoln and Theodore Roosevelt.

62-63 A panoramic view of the imposing Cliff Palace built by the Mesa Verdes in Colorado.

64 The small apartments at Mesa Verde were used mainly for storage and sleeping; communal life centered in open courts, rooftops and the well-like kivas.

65 The Mesa Verdes added to the Cliff Palace throughout their long occupation here.

66 *A kiva or ceremonial chamber for religious rituals addressed to the forces of nature and the spirits believed to indwell in every being.*

*67 Overhanging cliffs sheltered the Southwest's
pueblo Indians from the rigorous climate, with its
extremes of heat and cold.*

68 The Anasazi, forerunners of the pueblo culture, left ghostlike petroglyphs in the walls of Utah's caves and canyons.

69 The primitive beauty of Indian art is a bridge between the past and present of the West.

POOLS AND STREAMS

Yellowstone National Park lies on the Continental Divide, mainly on a mountain-surrounded plateau high in the Rocky Mountains. Within this region, where Wyoming touches on Montana and Idaho, rise the headstreams of rivers flowing to both the Atlantic and the Pacific—the Missouri and the Snake.

The thousand-mile Yellowstone River rises in the nearby Shoshone Mountains and flows north into the great Yellowstone Lake. Leaving the lake, the river cuts a deep gorge through this forested and sloping country, running ever deeper and faster until it thunders over the Upper Falls. For half a mile it gathers itself for the precipitous plunge over the 308-foot Lower Falls into the Grand Canyon of the Yellowstone. The river is named for the richly colored stone of the canyon's walls, which is stained by minerals in the hot water that seeps throughout this volcanic region. Its warm color changes subtly with the changing light of day.

When early explorers returned from Yellowstone with tales of smoking mountains, boiling springs, geysers and bubbling pits of mud, their stories were largely dismissed as typical frontier 'roarbacks.' Not until 1870 did a US government expedition verify the rumors that had circulated since John Colter split off from the Lewis and Clark Expedition and discovered what the itinerant trappers called 'Colter's Hell.' They became familiar with the region, but had no way of understanding its bizarre phenomena, caused by the earth's inner heat, which occurs very close to the surface here.

Over an extensive area of Yellowstone's 3400 square miles, hot water and gases rise to the surface from superheated magmas perhaps a mile below ground level. The soil is warm and even hot to the touch in these regions. Cold surface water seeping downward encounters the hot vapors and boils upward in the form of steam (fumaroles) or great geysers, of which the best known and most regular is Old Faithful, the park's emblem. It spouts thousands of gallons of hot water over 150 feet into the air about once an hour. Hundreds of other geysers send up their plumes and arcs of water at less regular intervals, accompanied by cannonading sounds within the earth that reverberate throughout the area day and night.

Jewel-like colored pools and sparkling terraces of travertine formed by hot springs dot the landscape. On the banks of the Firehole River, prevented from freezing by hot-water seepage, elks and bison can feed on the grass in deep winter. Wildlife abounds here, including moose, deer, bear, antelope and many smaller animals. Over 200 species of birds frequent the evergreen forests and numerous waterways of the park.

Only recently have hikers and riders penetrated deeply into Yellowstone's back country, far from the more-visited thermal attractions. Those who make the trek are rewarded by wide-open views of the rugged Absaroka Range, fields full of wildflowers and clear streams that widen into beaver ponds. Some lakes are so remote that they remain nameless and almost unvisited, serenely reflecting the clouds and peaks around them through the long summer days. The pools and streams of this part of Yellowstone are typical of the great Western wilderness of North America from the Yosemite Valley to British Columbia and Alberta.

71 Clypsedra Geyser leaps up from superheated underground chambers in the Yellowstone plateau.

72-73 The tall cone of Castle Geyser suggests that it is one of the oldest of Yellowstone's nearly 300 geysers.

74 Yellowstone's hot springs are brilliantly colored by a combination of minerals and tiny organisms—algae and bacteria—that thrive in water near boiling temperature.

75 top Mammoth Hot Springs has been formed by the evaporation of hot water seeping from the mountainside to form terraces of travertine.

75 bottom A distant view of Beauty Pool in Yellowstone's Upper Geyser Basin.

76 Visitors to Yellowstone await the irregular eruption of White Dome Geyser.

77 The eerie Fountain Paint Pot is formed by hot gases belching up through mud-filled pits to stain the mud with colored minerals.

78-79 The Emerald Pool is a gem-colored channel for hot water flowing steadily from the molten interior of the planet.

80-81 The algae-stained Opalescent Pool is rimmed by skeleton trees.

82-83 Mammoth Hot Springs is a fairy-tale setting constantly reshaped by its restless sculptor.

84 Ribbons of algae run through this fluid landscape.

85 Yellowstone National Park has the world's greatest concentration of thermal phenomena.

86-87 Explorers' tales of the wonders of Yellowstone were widely disbelieved until the region became more accessible.

88 The tranquil Merced River flows through Yosemite Valley, guarded by the granite monolith called El Capitan.

89 Thomas Wolfe said of Yellowstone, 'It is a fabulous country . . . the only place where miracles not only happen, but where they happen all the time.'

90 The glittering limestone steps of White Elephant Terrace at Mammoth Hot Springs.

91 Minerva Terrace, named for the goddess
whose magic shield turned enemies to stone.

SOARING STONE

One of the West's most compelling attractions is its incredible variety of sculptures in stone: spires and pinnacles carved by erosion; massive, sheer-sided monoliths split by glacial ice; soaring stone arches etched from solid rock by wind and frost. These formations appear ageless and immovable in their solidity, but like everything else in nature, they are still in process. The span of a single human life is simply too short to observe the infinitesimal changes wrought in stone by the relentless forces of running water, wind, ice and snow, and the restless movement of the earth itself.

Intuitively, man regards stones and rocks as a symbol of integrity and permanence. Primitive peoples saw them as the source of human life, while the soil—inferior because disintegrated— was regarded as the mother of vegetable and animal life. Stone seemed to be the very bones of the earth. Shrines and oracles have always been associated with caves and standing stones. Many cultures, including the Chinese, the Japanese and the American Indian, have ascribed a living spirit to stones, which still figure in the religious rituals of many lands.

In California's Yosemite Valley, on the western slope of the Sierra Nevada, South or Half Dome rises 5000 feet from the glacier-carved valley floor. Cathedral Rocks, opposite the granite vastness of El Capitan, and Glacier Point, command elevations of over 3000 feet. Utah's great Capitol Reef sandstone formations were a massive roadblock in the path of migrating settlers, but their disturbing beauty stirred unwilling admiration despite the obstacle they posed.

At Arches National Park, rocky canopies and slender stone bridges leap across deep canyons scoured out along faults in solid sandstone by wind and water. Vertical walls or fins remaining between these crevasses were affected by persistent weathering that worked away at the softer areas until it opened a small window that would eventually become a delicate arcade. Landscape Arch is a graceful ribbon of sandstone flung almost 300 feet across space: it seems impossible that this slender formation—at places only six feet wide—could defy the law of gravity by remaining upright. Some of the sculpted monoliths and spires here are the remnants of arches that have long since crumbled. Their shapes suggest both human and animal figures—the Three Gossips (or Graces, to the more poetically inclined); the Parade of Elephants, the Marching Men, Duck on a Rock. Twenty million years in the making, they are all in the slow process of dissolution into their constituent grains of sand.

Perhaps the grandest example of soaring stone in all the West is the great Rocky Mountain chain itself, North America's longest and highest mountain system. The Rockies are composed chiefly of granite and gneiss, but they embody a great variety of rocks, with occasional evidence of volcanic action, as in Yellowstone. Their rugged grandeur is equally awe-inspiring from the ground or from the air, whence the Continental Divide can be traced along their crest as far as the eye can see. Their naked summits and forested flanks inspire a sense of wonder that transcends anything we know about the geological forces that shaped them, and that will one day wear them away.

93 A grotesquely eroded rock formation dwarfs a resting traveler at Arches National Park.

94-95 Strange and beautiful monoliths rise from the floor of Monument Valley, on the border between Arizona and Utah.

96-97 Yosemite's massive Half Dome was sheared by icefields that undercut the great stone's upper layers when glaciers almost filled this valley.

98-99 A giant king beside his castle is only one of the identities suggested by this scene in Bryce Canyon.

100 More than 60 shades of red, pink, copper and cream appear in the canyon's bizarre formations.

101 A great slab of stone balances precariously atop a dome in California's Joshua Tree National Monument.

102-103 A nineteenth-century visitor described Arches as 'the work of giant hands.'

104-105 Isolated 'Delicate Arch' commands one of the most beautiful views of 115-square-mile Arches National Park.

106 Soaring 'Double Arch' was once part of a solid layer of smoky red sandstone.

107 These apparently permanent formations are
still subject to the continuous changes wrought
by weathering.

108 A ghostly desert shrub clings to life amid the boulders of Joshua Tree National Monument.

109 Cathedral-like columns of sandstone form a barrier that early Utah prospectors called a reef, at Capitol Reef National Park.

110-111 California's Red Rock Canyon is another chapter in the geological history recorded by the West's many-layered walls of stone.

112 Great capstones often top eroding 'stems' of
softer material that may finally snap under the load
they bear.

113 *An egg-shaped boulder of granite in the desert preserve at Joshua Tree National Monument.*

THE CANADIAN WEST

The untamed Rocky Mountains are among the greatest natural treasures of the West. They extend all the way from northern Alaska to America's Southwest, rising in Canada between Alberta, the westernmost Prairie Province, and British Columbia, the only Pacific Province and Canada's gateway to the Orient. Three of Alberta's five national parks—Banff, Jasper and Waterton Lakes—were created to preserve this region of jagged, snow-capped peaks; pristine lakes, many of which are tarns, scooped from the rock by glacial ice; and abundant wildlife of the field and forest.

Thick growths of aspen, balsam, fir, pine and spruce cover the northern foothills of the Rockies. The 100-square-mile Columbia Icefield, between Banff and Jasper, consists of huge glaciers from the Ice Age, some of whose frigid waters are carried to the Pacific by the surging rivers of British Columbia. At Waterton Lakes, ancient sedimentary rocks record a million years of geological history. This scenic area is part of the extensive Canadian-US International Peace Park.

Cerulean Lake Louise, with Victoria Glacier towering above it, is one of Alberta's most breathtaking sights. Other attractions include sandstone statuary, mineral hot springs, waterfalls and leaping mountain goats whose hooves disdain the most dizzying height for a point still higher. Visitors from all over the world are drawn here by the region's spectacular scenery, challenging peaks and year-round sporting activities.

On a brilliant summer day in the Canadian Rockies, it is hard to believe that winter winds above 200 miles an hour can scream across the timberline, twisting the limber pines into tortured shapes and driving all sentient life under shelter. Avalanches and rock falls are common, continuously changing the contours of the land. Snow may remain on the high subalpine meadows until midsummer, but the hardy, low-growing rock plants make little account of it. They have only weeks to germinate, flower and disseminate their seeds, and their greatest enemy is the dessicating wind. Their ground-hugging habit of growth allows them to conserve moisture as desert plants do. The short summer sees the brief but brilliant flowering of snow buttercups, yellow stonecrop, dwarf clovers and alpine forget-me-nots.

At lower elevations, the yellow violet and the wild rose flourish alongside pentstemons and blue columbine. Fast-growing, white-barked aspen must compete with the taller, longer-lived conifers for light. They are also a prime target for destruction by beavers, which prefer them above all other trees, both as food and as building material.

The Fraser River tumbles south and then west from the Rocky Mountains through British Columbia. The land it traverses is so rugged that explorer Simon Fraser and his party had to make frequent portages past falls and rapids like those of the Fraser's Big Canyon. The Canadian Pacific Railroad, too, had great difficulty in finding its way over and through what has been called 'a sea of mountains.' This vertical land remains little touched by the inroads of man, preserving itself as a wilderness stronghold over vast regions between the Rockies and the Coast Mountains. Beyond them are the prosperous coastal cities of Vancouver and Victoria and the fabled Inside Passage.

115 The incomparably beautiful setting of the Banff Springs Hotel, on the Bow River in the Canadian Rockies.

116 The turbulent Fraser River cuts a deep canyon through the wilds of western Canada on its drive toward the Pacific.

117 An alert mountain goat surveys its kingdom in the Canadian Rockies.

118-119 Spectral Sulphur Mountain looms above the jagged tree line in Banff National Park.

120 *The Athabasca River plunges over a great falls in its rush through the Rockies.*

121 *Mirror-like Maligne Lake in Alberta's Jasper National Park is a still point of beauty.*

122 The majestic Canadian Rockies etched in winter white.

123 The summit of Whistler's Mountain in Jasper National Park.

124-125 Idyllic Lake Louise, in Banff National Park, is Alberta's best-known lake.